Kids Gone Campin'

The Young Camper's Guide to Having More Fun Outdoors

Cherie Winner

Chanhassen, Minnesota

About the Author

Cherie Winner taught college zoology before starting her career as a writer. She enjoys camping and hiking with friends and with her dog, Sheba. Her previous children's books include *Penguins, Bison,* and *Lions* in the Our Wild World Series. She lives in Pullman, Washington.

Creative Publishing international

Copyright © 2006 by Creative Publishing international, Inc.

Creative Publishing international, Inc.
18705 Lake Drive East
Chanhassen, MN 55317
1-800-328-3895
www.creativepub.com

KIDS GONE CAMPIN'
by Cherie Winner

President/CEO: Ken Fund
Vice President/Publisher: Linda Ball
Vice President/Retail Sales & Marketing: Kevin Haas
Executive Editor, Outdoor Group: Barbara Harold
Creative Director: Brad Springer
Book Designer: Kari Johnston
Production Manager: Linda Halls
Illustrator: Tom Wallerick

Photographs © 2006: Aflo Agency/Alamy pp. 48; Cabela's pp. 22, 29, 45; Julie Caruso pp. 74, 80 (right); Chris Cheadle/Alamy pp. 4–5; Comstock Images/Alamy pp. 85; Creative Publishing international pp. 53, 80 (left); Steven A. Griffin pp. 13, 18, 28, 52, 60, 76, 87; Nick Hanna/Alamy pp. 64; Justin Kase/Alamy pp. 10; Robert Loewendick pp. 26, 40, 81 (left); Marge Meader pp. 36-37, 47; Edward Migdalski pp. 72; Tom Migdalski pp. 11, 58, 66, 69, 81 (right); Todd Pearson/CORBIS front cover; Photo Network/Alamy pp. 86; PhotoDisc, Inc./Getty pp. 82; Royalty-Free/CORBIS pp. 15, 23, 41; Rubberball/Alamy pp.19; Brad Springer pp. 31 (both), 51, 68, 75, 83 (bottom); Stock Connection/Alamy pp. 78–79; StockShot/Alamy pp. 16–17, 56–57; Swerve/Alamy pp. 12; Thinkstock/Alamy pp. 33, 44; TravelWisconsin.com pp. 13, 14, 83 (top).

Library of Congress Cataloging-in-Publication Data
Winner, Cherie.
  Kids gone campin' : the young camper's guide to having more fun outdoors / Cherie Winner.
    p. cm.
  Includes index.
  ISBN 1-58923-225-9 (soft cover)
  1. Camping--Handbooks, manuals, etc. 2. Outdoor recreation--Handbooks, manuals, etc. I. Title: Kids gone camping. II. Title.
  GV191.7.W57 2006
  796.54--dc22   2005023733

Printed in China
10 9 8 7 6 5 4 3 2 1

Gone Campin' Message

If you're like most kids who love the outdoors, you want to do more than go on picnics or hike a nature trail. You don't want to go home at the end of the day. You want to stay out in the woods, mountains, or desert. You want to camp.

By reading *Kids Gone Campin'*, you'll learn how to make roughing it easy. You'll find GREAT TIPS for choosing the best campsite and setting up your home away from home. You'll even find recipes for great fireside dishes.

It might take you a while to read this book, because it is filled with ideas for things to DO. You might stop reading right in the middle of a page, to go out and try a new camping skill. And that's great, because the better you get at those skills, the more fun you'll have on your camping adventure.

So read the tips, practice at home before you go, and then head for the great outdoors.

HAPPY CAMPING!

Contents

Where Can I GO?

No matter where you live, you'll find places to camp not far from your home. It may be a National Park with famous landmarks, a quiet camp-ground tucked among the trees, or even your own backyard.

The first part of this book shows you where to find good camping areas. It helps you decide whether to drive, hike, or paddle to your campsite. It also helps you plan your trip by choosing the best time to camp, and how long to stay.

TYPES OF LOCATIONS

Once you start looking for places to camp, you'll find them everywhere. Here are a few possibilities.

NATIONAL PARKS

National Parks are what a lot of people have in mind when they think of camping. They want to pitch a tent near Yellowstone's geysers or within shouting distance of the Grand Canyon. They want to dip a paddle in the waters of the Everglades, hike along a ridge in the Great Smoky Mountains, or wake to the sound of waves crashing on the shore of Isle Royale.

These parks are so popular that in summer and other prime times, you may need a reservation to get into the campgrounds. Plan ahead to be sure you can camp in the place you want.

National Parks also have miles of back country to explore. Hiking just a little way off the road gets you away from the crowds. Check in at the park office before heading into the wilderness. Most parks require you to tell them how many people are in your group, where you will camp, and when you expect to be back.

STATE PARKS

Every state in the U.S. has parks where you can camp, hike, fish, and go boating. These are great places to camp when you don't have time to go on a long trip to a distant area.

In a state park, you'll probably stay in a campground that has fire rings and grills, outhouses, trash bins, and drinkable water. State parks usually aren't big enough to have back-country or wilderness camping.

National Parks

NATIONAL FORESTS

National Forests are vast areas in every state where people can get out and enjoy the natural world. Some are filled with towering trees. Others don't look like forests at all. They are in the desert or along the seashore. No matter what they look like, they all have great places to pitch your tent.

National Forest campgrounds have outhouses, trash bins, and a water pump. There may even be a "campground host" who lives there full-time and can tell you the best places to hike or fish nearby.

You don't have to stay in a campground, though. Most National Forests have places where you can pull off the road and set up camp on your own. Campsites like this don't have an outhouse, so you'll have to make a latrine. And they don't have a pump, so you'll have to bring your own water or purify stream water before drinking it. But you will probably have the place all to yourself.

If you want to try this kind of camping, look for a spot where other campers have stayed before. If there's already a fire ring at the site, use it. Don't disturb other areas by making a new campsite or a new fire ring.

National Forests

COMMERCIAL CAMPGROUNDS

A commercial campground, run by private citizens as a business, will probably have bathrooms (with showers!), drinking water, and trash bins. It may even have a convenience store and a swimming pool.

These are great places for first-time campers, families, or people who aren't comfortable being out in the wild.

Many commercial campgrounds are designed for big recreational vehicles. They are paved and feel more like a parking lot than a campground. If you just want a place to park for the night, they are OK. If you want to get closer to nature, they may not be a good choice.

Some commercial campgrounds are quieter, with lots of trees and smaller campsites. They are just right for campers with a tent or small trailer.

YOUR OWN BACKYARD

Your own yard is a great place to camp. You can practice all your tent-pitching, campfire-building, and sleeping-in-a-bag skills just a short distance from your own back door. If the tent falls down or a thunderstorm blows through, you can go back in the house and get warm and dry.

Besides, camping in your own backyard can be a big adventure. You'll see your neighborhood in a very different way after spending the night outside. You might see bats zooming overhead, or hear an owl hooting softly in the distance.

HOW DO I GET THERE?

Some ways of reaching your campsite are a lot more challenging than others. Choose a way that fits your skills and will be the most fun for you.

CAR CAMPING

Car camping doesn't mean you sleep in your car, although you can, if you want to. It means you set up camp close to your car. Most campgrounds are like this. You drive in and park next to your campsite.

When you go car camping, you can take lots of gear, clothing, and food. You can even take heavy items like canned applesauce or pork and beans. This is probably the best way to start camping.

TRAILERS

Many families camp in a trailer. Some trailers have hard sides, so they're like cabins on wheels. Others have a pop-up tent you unfold when you reach your campsite.

Trailers offer more comfortable beds than tent camping, and better protection against rain, wind, and cold.

They also have a refrigerator, so you can take along foods that need to stay cold. Some even include a bathroom.

If you and your family think you might like trailer camping, you can try it out by renting a trailer for a week or two.

BACKPACKING AND CANOEING

Backpacking and canoeing require special equipment and skills, but they can take you farther into the wilderness than you can go by car. Almost every National Forest and National Park has trails to camping spots deep in the back country. Many have water routes along rivers or lakes. Ask forest rangers or camping guides about the best routes and campsites.

When you backpack, you carry all of your gear and food. That means taking just the lightest and most necessary stuff.

When you canoe camp, you can take a lot of gear as long as it's waterproof. Chances are, it will get wet sometime during the trip.

You may encounter "portages" where you have to carry your canoe and your gear over land to reach the next stretch of open water. Before you head out on a canoe camping trip, find out where the portages are and how long it will take you to make them.

WHEN SHOULD I GO?

Of course, you should go camping as often as you like!
But some times are better than others.

SEASONS

You can camp in any season, as
long as you're prepared for
the weather. Each season has
special attractions—different
things to do while you're
camping. As a beginning
camper, stick with spring,
summer, or fall camping.
If you camp in winter,
you'll need a more expensive
sleeping bag and tent, and
special clothing that will
keep you warm even if it gets wet.

WEEKEND OR WEEKDAY

Campgrounds are busiest on weekends and holidays.
If the campground is crowded, the fishing spots and
hiking trails will be crowded, too. Try to make your
trip at less busy times.

When you're planning your trip, call the campground
to see if you need to reserve a spot. If you're going
to a place that doesn't take reservations, don't wait
until dinner time to start looking for a good spot.
Find a campsite in the afternoon.

HOW LONG DO I STAY?

You can camp for a night, a weekend, a week, or longer. If you're new to camping, start with short trips. As you get better at camp craft, you will probably want to stay out longer.

If your trip lasts more than a day, you'll have a choice. You can stay in one camp and take field trips each day to hike, fish, or explore the area around your camp. In the afternoon you return to your camp, which is already set up. Or, you can move camp every day or two. In the morning you'll strike camp (take it down) and pack your gear. Then it's off down the trail or down the river. Later in the day, you'll find a new campsite and set up your tent and kitchen again.

Some campers like to move camp every day. Others like to stay put and explore the area around one campsite. Try both, and find out which way you like best.

What Gear Do I Need?

Whatever kind of camping you do, you will need the right gear to stay warm, dry, and well fed. If you go car camping or backyard camping, you can take more and heavier gear. If you hike to your campsite, you'll want to take as light a load as possible. If you travel by canoe, your load can be somewhere in between.

In this chapter, you'll find out what gear you'll need to create your own bedroom, kitchen, and bathroom in the wild.

TENTS

Your tent is more than a place to sleep. If the weather turns nasty during your trip, the tent will also be your family room and dining room. When you shop for a tent, get inside it and imagine living in it for a few days. Could you easily change clothes in it? Could you sit up in it to eat or play a game with your tent-mates? Choose a tent you feel comfortable in.

SIZES

The label on a tent might say "2-man," "3-man," or "4-man," but check for yourself. If you're looking for a 3-person tent, put yourself, two friends, and three sleeping bags in the tent. Do you have enough room? If you think you'd feel cramped in the 3-man tent, get the 4-man tent instead.

THE FLY

The fly is a waterproof sheet that shields the tent from rain. It hangs a few inches above the sides and top of the tent. The gap between the fly and the tent lets air circulate around the tent. That helps the tent stay cool in hot weather and warm in cool weather.

TENT SEASONS

A SUMMER TENT has many mesh windows for ventilation, a light color to reflect heat from the sun, and a small fly that covers the top half of the tent.

A 3-SEASON TENT has good ventilation, a light or medium color, and a waterproof floor. Its fly covers most of the tent, for good protection against rain.

A 4-SEASON TENT has more support poles, a dark color to absorb heat from the sun, and a fly that goes almost all the way to the ground. This is really a cold-weather tent. You'd roast in a tent like this on a summer trip.

Pole-supported

POLE-SUPPORTED VS. SELF-SUPPORTING

A POLE-SUPPORTED TENT is held up by ropes tied to trees or poles stuck in the ground. Once you set it up, it's rooted to that spot. If you want to move it, you have to completely take it down and start from scratch in the new location.

A SELF-SUPPORTING TENT is held up by a framework of poles that attach to loops on the tent and that are held together by elastic "shock cords." You can set up this tent in one spot, and then pick it up and move it to another spot.

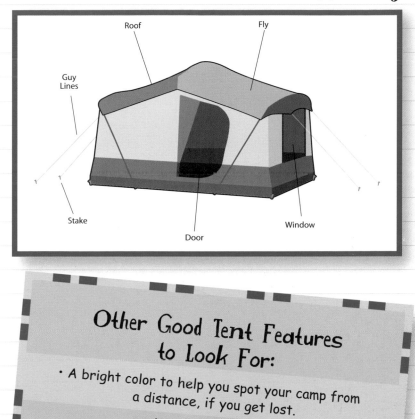

Roof Fly

Guy
Lines

Stake

Door

Window

Other Good Tent Features to Look For:

- A bright color to help you spot your camp from a distance, if you get lost.

- Waterproof floor.

- Sides and top breathable, not waterproof.

- Fire-retardant fabric.

- Windows covered with mesh to let in air and keep out bugs.

- Solid window flaps that zip shut for privacy.

- Strong, easy-to-work zipper, size 8 or 10.

- Stakes to anchor the tent to the ground after it is set up.

TARPS

A tarp is a waterproof cloth made of plastic, oiled canvas, or nylon. A plastic tarp is lightest and easiest to handle. It should be at least 8 feet (2.5 m) square. A tarp with grommets—holes lined with metal rims—is easier to tie to trees or stakes than a plain tarp.

Tarps are so handy in camp that you might want to take several. Use them to cover your eating area, the gap between two tents, and as a pad to sit on when the ground is damp. Carry a tarp with you on long hikes. It will make a great emergency tent if you get lost or can't get back to camp before nightfall.

In wet weather, put one underneath the tent and another one inside. The tarp inside the tent can be a bit bigger than the floor, so it comes a few inches up the sides of the tent. The tarp under your tent should be a bit smaller than the floor of the tent. You shouldn't be able to see it when the tent is set up. If it extends past the tent floor, rainwater can drip off the fly onto the tarp, and then run underneath the tent. Squish!

Look for a bag that fits you and the kind of camping you plan to do. When you find a bag that looks good, take it off the rack. Lay it on the floor, get into it, and zip it up. Stay in it for at least 5 minutes, in your normal sleeping position. Is it too snug? Maybe you want to be able to spread out more. Is it too loose? Maybe you like having your covers tucked in around you. Find a bag that feels just right.

Whatever kind of bag you get, choose one that's just a bit longer than you are tall. If it's a lot longer, you'll have trouble staying warm in it because your body will have to heat up more extra space.

SHAPES

A MUMMY BAG has a hood that closes with a draw-string, so only your face shows, like a mummy. It fits you so snugly that it moves with you whenever you curl up or roll over.

A SEMI-MUMMY BAG has more room than a mummy bag. It lets you roll over and move around inside it.

A RECTANGULAR BAG gives you the most room inside, but it is bigger and heavier than other styles of bags. It's a great choice for car camping.

Mummy Bag

Semi-mummy Bag

Rectangular Bag

Sleeping Pad

Pillow

FILLINGS

Sleeping bags are filled with fibers that puff up and insulate you against the cold. How much the fibers puff up is called the "loft." A higher loft number means a better-quality bag. Get a bag with a loft of at least 550.

The fibers can be either natural down (very fine feathers) or synthetic (man-made). Goose down is the lightest and warmest filling. However, it is expensive, and it doesn't insulate if it gets wet. Synthetic fillings weigh more than goose down, but they insulate well even if they get wet. They also cost less.

COMFORT RATING

The comfort rating of a sleeping bag tells you the coldest temperature at which the bag will keep you warm. Find out how cold the nights are likely to be when you camp. Look for a bag rated for about 10°F (18°C) less than that.

Don't get a colder-rated bag if you won't need it. A winter-rated bag will be way too hot in warm seasons.

A bag rated at 50°F (10°C) will work fine for summer camping in a warm climate. A bag rated at 20 to 25°F (-6.7 to -3.9°C) will be good for camping in spring, summer, or fall.

SLEEPING PADS

A sleeping pad is placed between your bag and the ground. It softens the ground and evens out the bumps. It also insulates the side of you that's next to the ground.

A couple of old blankets make a great pad. If you need a lighter pad, choose one of these:

- closed-cell foam—lightweight and waterproof, but firm and bulky.

- open-cell foam—softer than closed-cell, but it absorbs water, so get one that's covered with a waterproof fabric.

- self-inflating—great for any kind of camping. You open the valve, and it inflates itself. Get one that's covered with a rough fabric so you don't slip off it during the night.

WHAT ABOUT AN AIR MATTRESS?

An air mattress is a poor choice for any kind of camping. It's hard to inflate and easy to tear. One of the other kinds of pads will be warmer and softer, and will last longer.

WHAT ABOUT A PILLOW?

You can take your favorite pillow from home, or use a towel or shirt to cushion your head.

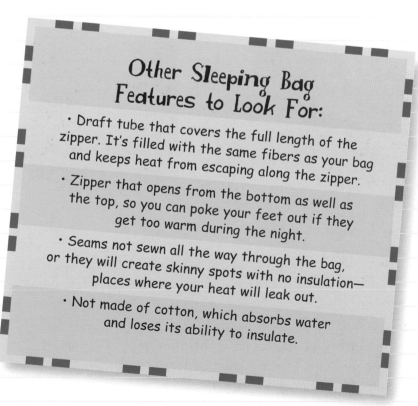

Other Sleeping Bag Features to Look For:

- Draft tube that covers the full length of the zipper. It's filled with the same fibers as your bag and keeps heat from escaping along the zipper.
- Zipper that opens from the bottom as well as the top, so you can poke your feet out if they get too warm during the night.
- Seams not sewn all the way through the bag, or they will create skinny spots with no insulation— places where your heat will leak out.
- Not made of cotton, which absorbs water and loses its ability to insulate.

THE CAMP KITCHEN

Your kitchen area in camp is almost as important as where you sleep. After all, when you get back to camp after an afternoon of swimming or wildlife-watching, you'll be HUNGRY.

A well-stocked kitchen can make the difference between a camping trip that's just OK, and one that's really FANTASTIC!

POTS AND PANS

Take a frying pan at least 10 inches (25 cm) across and a 1-quart (1 l) sauce pan for every 3 to 4 campers. Look for pans with lids, a nonstick surface, and no handles. Get a special "gripper" handle made just for campers. It lets you pick up any pan. The pans, lids, and gripper handle should all be made of metal. Don't get the very lightest pans you find. They will heat up so fast your food will scorch.

A reflector oven lets you make brownies and other baked goods. The oven is a shiny box you set on top of hot coals or a stove burner. Put your batter inside, set it on the fire, and get ready for a real treat.

Some campers use a Dutch oven, a large cast-iron pot you bury in coals. Dutch ovens do a great job, but they are heavy and a little hard to handle. You might want to borrow one to try it out before buying one of your own.

COOKING UTENSILS

Be sure to take these: a spatula, a big cooking spoon, tongs, and a long cooking fork. Their handles should be made of metal or wood. Plastic handles melt if you accidentally leave the utensil in a cooking pan.

Other items to put in your kitchen kit are: a can opener, a paring knife, and pot holders.

TABLEWARE

Each camper should have these items: a deep plate that can also be used as a bowl, a large cup or mug, and a fork, spoon, and table knife. All plates, cups, and utensils should be made of metal.

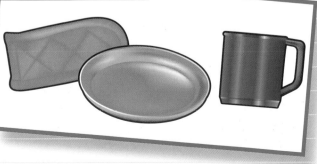

COOKSTOVES

Because there may not be cooking facilities where you camp, it's always a good idea to take a stove with you. You might not be able to make a campfire because of fire danger, lack of wood, or stormy weather. Most stoves light with a match, but some new models have an electronic starter that works even in a pouring rain.

If you're going to backpack, find a small, lightweight stove. It will probably have just one burner. You'll have to cook one-pot meals, or cook and eat one dish at a time.

If you can take a heavier stove, a two-burner Coleman will let you cook a whole meal at once. If you camp with a large group, you might want a 3-burner stove or two 2-burner stoves. Look for a stove that can use more than one kind of fuel (only one kind at a time, though!).

Common fuels include propane, Coleman fuel, and unleaded automobile gas.

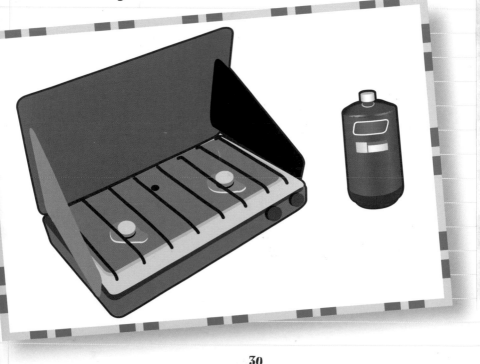

Whatever kind of fuel you use, be sure your stove's tank is full before you head out. Use a funnel to pour the fuel. Write "stove fuel" on the funnel with permanent ink, so you don't accidentally use it for water.

FOOD AND WATER STORAGE

Sealable sandwich bags and plastic snap-top containers are great for carrying solid foods. They're also handy for holding things like matches and toilet paper. Liquids travel well in wide-mouth bottles with screw tops. Label all your containers so you'll know what's inside them. Many camp foods look alike until you cook them.

Each camper will carry a canteen or water bottle, but the kitchen should also have a water supply you can all draw from. Take a plastic jug that holds from 2 to 5 gallons (7.5 to 19 l) and has a wide-mouth screw cap at the top and a spigot near the bottom.

CLEANUP

A plastic dishpan makes a good sink. Take a nylon scrubby and some grease-cutting dish soap that is biodegradable. For trash, take heavy-duty garbage bags.

BATHROOM SUPPLIES

If you won't be near an outhouse, take a folding camp shovel to dig a latrine. If you don't want to dig a latrine, take a portable toilet. It's a box with a tank inside and a toilet seat on top. Take along a bottle of toilet chemicals that will help break down the wastes and keep the tank from smelling bad.

Take at least one roll of toilet paper for every three campers for every day of the trip. It's not a good idea to use leaves or sticks instead of toilet paper. You could get a nasty infection. Use toilet paper, and dispose of it properly.

Waterless hand sanitizer is better to clean with than soap, because you don't have to rinse it off. Take several small bottles rather than one big one, so every camper can carry one in a pocket or day pack.

Each camper should have his or her own washcloth and towel.

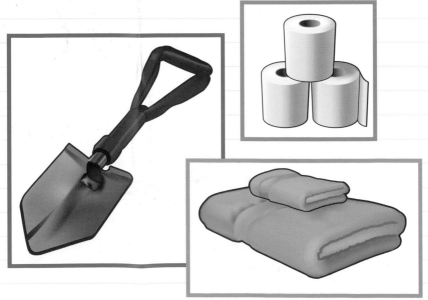

Take a small, powerful flashlight and an extra set of batteries for it. Some flashlights clip onto a shirt or headband so your hands are free.

A lantern is a great addition to any camp. After the fire has died down, or on nights when you don't make a fire, a lantern lets you see what you're doing. If you have a battery-powered lantern, take a spare battery. If it's fuel-powered, get one that uses the same fuel as your cookstove so you can fill both from the same source.

Take a good first-aid kit that includes adhesive bandages, antibiotic cream, tweezers for pulling out splinters and ticks, aspirin or acetaminophen, and anti-diarrheal medicine.

Pack plenty of sunscreen, bug repellent, and lip balm, too—and remember to use them!

ODDS & ENDS

You'll need just a few other items to make your camping adventure run smoothly.

Always carry a POCKET KNIFE. It doesn't have to be big. A 2- to 3-inch (5- to 7.5-cm) blade is perfect. A knife that has tools like a screwdriver, a saw, and tweezers is one of the best items you can take to camp.

Carry a WHISTLE at all times. You can use it to call for help if you get lost or hurt.

A TROWEL OR FOLDING SHOVEL helps spread dirt on a fire, and it's absolutely necessary if you're going to be digging a latrine.

A FOLDING SAW can be used to cut firewood to the right length for your fire. A HATCHET splits thick logs into chunks that are easier to burn.

If your MATCHES aren't waterproof, put them in a container that is. Also take about two dozen COTTON FIREBALLS (from the cosmetics section of a store)

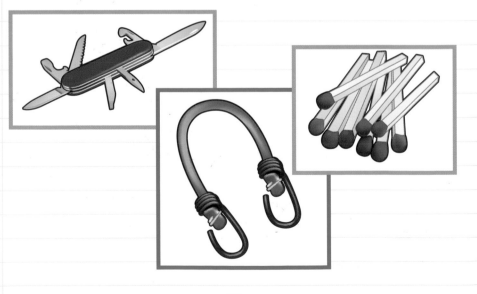

that you have coated with petroleum jelly. They'll help you start a fire in any kind of weather.

Take a few BUNGEE CORDS with hooks on the ends, and several yards (meters) of ROPE OR TWINE that is strong enough to hold up your tarp. For emergency repairs of ripped clothing or tents, take WAXED DENTAL FLOSS and a SEWING NEEDLE with an eye big enough for the floss. Dental floss is incredibly strong, and the waxed kind is waterproof.

Finally, make a checklist of all your supplies and equipment. Use it when you load up for your trip, so you won't forget something important.

WHERE DO I PUT ALL THAT STUFF?

If you just toss all these items in the car, you'll have a terrible mess. Carry them in plastic snap-top boxes, separated by function. You might keep your stove, cooking utensils, and dishes in one box. All foods go in another. The tools and ropes could go in a third. Then, when you need a particular item, you will know which box to look in to find it.

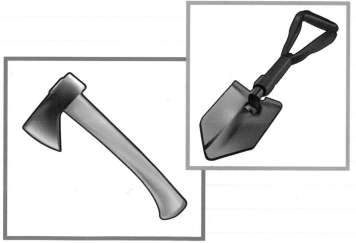

How Do
I Make
Camp?

Y ou have all your gear and
you found a great area to
explore. Now what? All that
preparation won't mean anything
if you don't know what to do once
you get to camp.

In this chapter, you'll learn how
to turn all that cool gear into a
safe, comfortable home away
from home.

CHOOSING A SITE

Find a spot that's the right distance away from the source of water and from the outhouse (or latrine). You want to be close enough that you can easily bring water to your camp, and won't have too long a walk to reach the outhouse—especially if you have to get up in the middle of the night!

Don't get too close, though. If you're too close to a stream, your campsite might flood. It will also be 10 to 15°F (5.5 to 8.3°C) colder than sites farther from the stream.

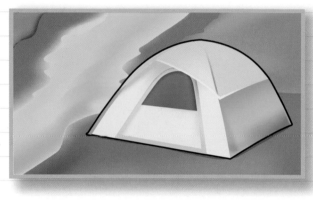

If you're too close to a pump or the outhouse, you'll hear traffic as everyone else tromps by on their way to use the facilities.

Look for possible dangers. Don't pitch your tent in a gully that might flood, or at the base of a cliff where rocks might fall on it. Don't pitch your tent under a tree with dead limbs that might break off in a high wind, or under the only tall tree around. It could attract lightning.

How close is the site to other campers? You might like having close neighbors, or you might prefer to have more privacy.

Make sure your site is flat and level. If it slopes a bit, position your tent so your head will be above your feet. The ground should be smooth, with no rocks or tree roots sticking out.

The site should have a fire ring where you can build a campfire or set up your cookstove. It can be about 10 feet (3 m) in diameter. There should be bare dirt or rock for several feet around the fire ring,

and no branches hanging low over it. If you can, find out what direction the wind usually blows. Place your tent upwind of the fire, so you won't breathe in the smoke from your own campfire.

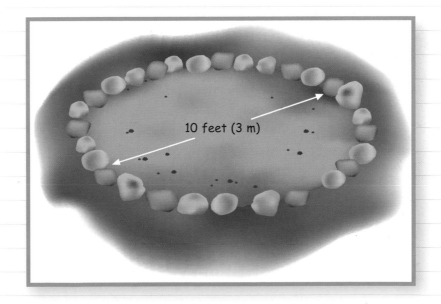

10 feet (3 m)

PITCHING THE TENT

Practice pitching your tent at home. The first time you pitch a new tent is usually the hardest. After that, it gets easier. (One tip: close the tent's zippers before setting it up.) Keep practicing. When you can set up your tent in the dark, during a rainstorm, with the wind blowing, you will be real pro!

If your tent is pole-supported, be sure you drive the poles deep enough into the ground that they won't fall over. Whether your tent is pole-supported or self-supporting, stake it in place. Otherwise, a strong wind could blow it away—with you inside!

Stakes are pegs about 1 foot (30 cm) long, made of wood, plastic, or metal. Pound the sharp end into the ground close to your tent, so the stake tilts away from the tent. Then tie or clip a cord from the tent to the stake. Use one stake

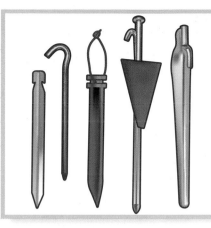

at each corner and at least one on each side of your tent. Use more if the wind is strong.

Years ago, campers were told to dig a narrow trench around their tent to drain off rain water. Modern tents and flies are good at keeping the rain out, and trenching makes campsites messy and muddy for everyone. So, don't trench.

MAKING YOUR BED

Unroll your sleeping bag and shake it so the filling can fluff up. Unroll your pad and let it expand, too.

Every morning, unzip your bag and gently shake it to fluff it up. Drape it over a log or rock, or lay it on the ground outside the tent to air it out, for at least half an hour.

FINAL PREPARATIONS

Set out your lantern and flashlights where they will be easy to find when it starts getting dark.

Go to the pump to fill your water jug. If your campground doesn't have a pump, purify a few gallons of river or lake water for your kitchen jug.

If your campground has an outhouse, be sure you know where it is. If not, prepare your latrine.

Walk around the campground and get acquainted with your new neighborhood.

The best camping trips are safe camping trips. Getting hurt or sick is no fun at all. Here are some suggestions to make your camping trip the best ever:

- Be smart in your choice of campsite. Don't pitch your tent in a gully, at the base of a cliff, or under a tall tree.

- Make your fire in an established fire ring or pit. Don't make a big fire that sends sparks flying a long distance away. Keep flammable items several feet (meters) away from the fire. Before you leave the campsite or turn in for the night, be sure the fire is completely out.

- Take along a good first-aid kit. If you can, take a class in first aid before your trip.

- Whenever you leave the campground, go with a buddy. Don't wander off by yourself. If you think you might be lost, stop walking. Use your whistle (if you brought one) or yell for help.

- Be careful when handling knives, tent stakes, or any-thing else with a sharp edge or point. Keep the sharp parts pointed away from yourself and other people.

- Use plenty of high-SPF sunscreen and a good bug repellent.

- Use water that comes from an approved tap or that you have purified.

- Avoid dangerous animals and plants.

THINGS TO WATCH OUT FOR

When you camp, it's a good idea to stay on the trail. You might encounter plants or animals that aren't much fun to be around. Here are some tips about how to avoid them and what to do if you can't.

POISON IVY, POISON OAK, AND POISON SUMAC

If you touch these plants, they will make you break out in itchy hives. Learn what they look like. Scout the area around your campsite and make a note of any you see growing. Tell your fellow campers so they don't accidentally run into it.

If you get the hives, they will itch like crazy. Try not to scratch. Calamine lotion or anti-itch cream can reduce the itch.

BUGS

Use bug repellent to keep mosquitoes and biting flies away. Long sleeves and pants help, too. An "itch stick" of anti-itch medicine comes in a tube like lip balm. Rub it on a bug bite to make the itch go away.

Tick bites aren't so itchy, but some ticks can carry Lyme disease and Rocky Mountain spotted fever. To keep ticks off you, spray bug repellent on your pants legs and socks, and check your clothing and skin (all over!) at least twice a day. Ticks usually wander around on a person for a few hours before they bite, so if you catch them early, you can avoid being bitten. If you brought pets, be sure to watch for ticks on them, too.

If a tick has clamped down on you, ask an adult for help to remove it. If you pull it out too fast, its head may stay attached to your skin. Use tweezers to grab the tick's head, as close to your skin as you can. Then pull slowly. You'll feel a little pop when it comes out.

Bees usually aren't a problem, but if you are allergic to bee stings, take along an adrenaline kit in case you get stung.

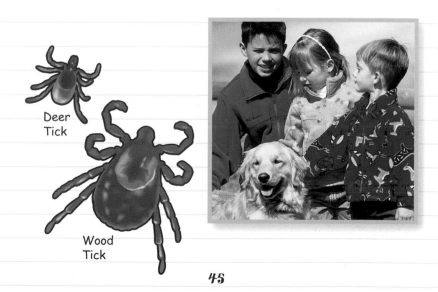

Deer
Tick

Wood
Tick

SNAKES

If you see a snake, don't try to catch it. Give it a chance to get out of your way. There are only a few kinds of snakes in the U.S. and Canada that are very dangerous. Coral snakes have bright yellow, black, and red bands around the body. They look like king snakes, which are harmless, except the bands are in a different order. There's a rhyme that tells you which is which, but if you meet a snake that's yellow, black, and red, you probably will be so excited and scared you won't be able to remember it. It's easier to just avoid the snake.

The other dangerous species are copperheads, water moccasins, and rattlesnakes. All have a thick body, a head shaped like a triangle, and a pit on each side of the face between the eye and the nostril. If you see any of those features, turn and go the other way.

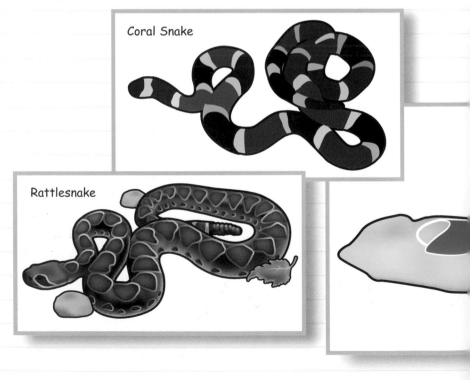

Coral Snake

Rattlesnake

BEARS

If you plan to camp in bear country, find out what you should do to prepare. In some areas with bears, only hard-sided trailers are allowed. No tents. The campground may have a flyer about how to act in bear country. Be sure to read it. Follow the rules. They are there to keep you safe.

RACCOONS

A raccoon begging for food might look cute, but it can give you a nasty bite. Don't offer it food. Be sure you dispose of all your trash in a racoon-proof container.

SLEEPING WELL

ON A WARM NIGHT, YOU CAN STAY COOLER IF
YOU DO THESE THINGS:

- Line your bag with a cotton sheet. Hang the sheet
  outside during the day to let it air out.

- Leave your bag unzipped.

- Open the tent window flaps to let the breeze
  blow through.

- Sleep on top of the bag rather than inside it.

ON A COLD NIGHT, YOU CAN STAY WARMER IF
YOU DO THESE THINGS:

- Protect your tent from wind by placing it on the east or south side of trees.

- Line your bag with a flannel sheet or a thin blanket. Air out the sheet or blanket during the day.

- Wear a cap, socks, long johns, and a fleece jacket to bed.

- Do a few jumping jacks before going to bed. This generates heat in your body, which can then warm up the sleeping bag.

- Eat a high-energy snack or drink something hot just before going to bed. Cocoa, soup, or hot water do a great job of warming you up from the inside. Don't drink so much that you'll have to get up in the middle of the night to go to the bathroom. Then you'll have to warm up your bed all over again.

WHERE DO I GO TO THE BATHROOM?

If there's an outhouse at your camp, use it. Take your own toilet paper, in case the outhouse runs out. Keep a roll of it in a waterproof bag in your tent, where you can easily find it if you have to get up in the middle of the night.

PORTABLE TOILET

If you take a portable toilet, set it on level ground several yards (meters) from your tent. Hang a tarp from trees to give some privacy. Hang a roll of toilet paper on a branch or a stick stuck in the ground. On your way home, empty the toilet at an RV dump site.

LATRINE

If there's no outhouse or portable toilet, you'll have to dig a latrine. This is sometimes called a cat hole. Choose a site at least 100 yards (90 m) from any stream or lake, so your waste doesn't seep through the soil and pollute the water.

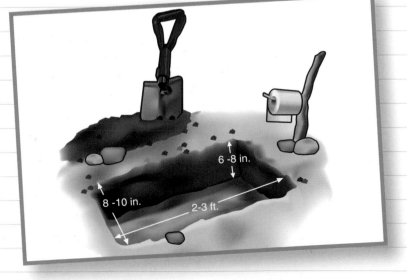

8 -10 in.

6 -8 in.

2-3 ft.

With your camp shovel, dig a trench 6 to 8 inches (15 to 20 cm) deep, 8 to 10 inches (20 to 25 cm) wide, and 2 to 3 feet (60 to 90 cm) long. Pile the dug-up dirt alongside the trench.

When you use the latrine, start at the far end, so the open trench is in front of you. When you're done, put your toilet paper in the trench with your waste. Cover it all with dirt. The next person uses the part of the trench just in front of the area you used. When one trench is filled in, dig another one several yards (meters) from the first.

KEEPING CLEAN

Wash your hands after going to the bathroom and before you handle food or drinking water. Use a no-water antibacterial soap. You use it like liquid soap, but it doesn't lather and doesn't need to be rinsed off.

Wash other parts of yourself with a washcloth and warm water. For a real treat on a long camping trip, pack a solar shower, which is a black plastic bag with

a hook on the top and a nozzle at the bottom. Fill it with water and hang it in the sun while you go off to hike or fish. When you come back a few hours later, the water will be warm. Put up a tarp for privacy, open the nozzle, and enjoy your shower.

WHERE DO I GET WATER?

You might be tempted to take a drink from a clear, cold stream or lake. Don't! Here's how to get a safe drink of water.

PUMP OR FAUCET

The easiest place to get water is a pump or faucet. There should be a sign near it that says the water is "potable," or safe to drink.

Many campers run to the pump with a bucket every time they need a little water. A better way is to fill up a big jug as soon as you set up camp, and use that for all your cooking and drinking water.

While other campers are waiting in line at the pump before dinner, you'll already have the water you need close at hand.

Refill your jug whenever you see it is less than one-third full.

STREAMS AND LAKES

Natural water looks so fresh. Why not get your drinking water there? Because even fresh-looking water can contain microbes that can make you very sick. You can use natural water in camp, and sometimes you have to because there is no other source. But you must first treat it to make it safe. Don't drink water straight out of a river or lake.

Giardia (pronounced gee-AR-dee-uh) is the microbe that causes the most problems for careless campers. It lives in natural waters. If it gets into you, you won't know it right away. Two to three weeks later, you'll suffer awful cramps and diarrhea. You can avoid this nasty bug by drinking water that comes from approved taps or that you have purified.

WATER TREATMENT

There are three ways to make natural water safe to drink:

- Use a water purifier. Collect water in a jug or pot. Let it sit for an hour or until most of the dirt particles settle to the bottom. Keep the purifier's "In" hose off the bottom so it doesn't slurp up any of the dirt. If the water is still cloudy, use a rubber band to attach a coffee filter to the tip of the "In" hose. Write down how much water you pump through your purifier so you will know when to replace the filter.

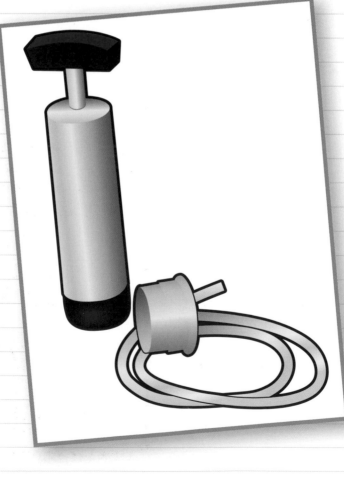

- Boil it. Bring the water to a full boil—bubbling and rolling in the pot. Keep it boiling for 3 to 5 minutes. Then let it cool (if you want to drink it), or add it to your cook pot (if you want to use it to prepare a meal). Purify your water before mixing it with food.

- Add iodine tablets, liquid, or powder to the water. Follow the directions that come with the iodine. Be sure the water is at least 69°F (20.5°C) when you treat it, or the iodine won't kill the microbes. Let the iodine work for at least half an hour. Then you can drink the water. You might want to add neutralizer tablets first to get rid of the iodine taste.

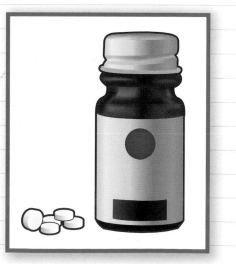

What Will I Eat?

Some campers just toss a lot of food in the car and head for the hills. If you don't care much about what you eat, that works fine. But with a little planning, you can eat as well in camp as you do at home.

If you're camping with a trailer or near your car, you can use canned foods and other heavy items. If you're traveling light, you'll want to use mainly dehydrated (dried) foods. They don't weigh much and they pack into a small space. When you add water to them, they swell up and look like normal food again. Even drinks come dried! Powdered lemonade, hot chocolate mix, and fruit juices are great additions to the camping pantry.

What Will I Eat? (cont.)

Sporting goods stores carry foods that were made especially for campers, but you will find plenty of good choices at a regular grocery store. Tuna and salmon now come in lightweight pouches rather than heavy cans. Cornbread mix, brownie mix, dehydrated soups, pasta, and powdered pasta sauces work great in camp.

Biscuit mix, sugar, salt, pepper, powdered milk, powdered eggs, dehydrated onion flakes, and dehydrated green vegetables are staples you can use in many different dishes. You can also add mustard, ketchup, and mayonnaise in single-serving packets. You can even take a sealed container of margarine, which does not have to be refrigerated as butter does.

You can plan on eating about half again as much as you eat at home. If you eat a cup (225 g) of cereal for breakfast at home, you'll probably want 1-1/3 to 1-1/2 cups (290 to 340 g) of cereal in camp.

Make a list of the meals you'll need each day of your trip. Then write down what you want to eat for each meal. Here's a sample menu for one day in camp:

Breakfast:

- instant oatmeal with hot fruit compote
- scrambled eggs made with dehydrated eggs and bacon bits
- juice

Lunch:

- peanut butter and jelly sandwiches
- potato chips
- fruit roll-ups
- brownies

Dinner:

- vegetable soup
- macaroni & cheese with ham
- pudding

DON'T FORGET SNACKS!

Dried fruits and fruit roll-ups, power bars, non-melting candy, crackers, and chips taste great and keep your stomach from growling. Gorp, or trail mix, is a great choice. You can buy gorp ready-made, or you can make your own. Mix salted nuts, raisins, dates, sunflower seeds, or any other small dried foods you like. Package your gorp in small sealable bags, one bag per day per person.

Of course, you can also pick wild berries, nuts, and seeds to eat—be sure you know which ones are safe.

Here are a few tasty dishes you can easily cook while camping:

Fish

If you go fishing and catch your dinner, try cooking it in different ways. A simple and tasty way is to fry it in a pan with butter, salt, and pepper. Try lemon pepper to give it a more tangy flavor, or Cajun seasonings to make it spicy.

Mac and Cheese Plus

Follow the directions on the Mac & Cheese box, and add tuna fish, chopped ham, or cut-up hot dogs. You can also add a vegetable, such as chopped broccoli, peas, or green beans. Stir in some mustard or sprinkle a little Parmesan cheese on it for extra flavor.

You can do the same thing with a package of scalloped or au gratin potatoes.

Biscuits and Dumplings

Take plenty of biscuit mix, which you can use to make pancakes, biscuits, stew dumplings, sweet dumplings, and more. Follow the directions on the box. Substitute powdered milk and powdered eggs for fresh milk and eggs.

Fruit Compote

Cover 1 cup (250 ml) of dried fruit (apples, peaches, cranberries, bananas, prunes, etc.) with water. Put a lid on the container and let it sit for several hours.

Eat it plain or on top of pancakes, or set it on the fire and cook it for 10-20 minutes. Use the compote instead of water to prepare instant oatmeal or another hot cereal. Or plop sweet dumpling dough on it, cook it until the dumplings are done, and you'll have a yummy cobbler.

S'mores

For each serving, you'll need:

2 square graham crackers

1 square of chocolate bar big enough to almost cover the graham cracker

1 big marshmallow

Put the chocolate on a graham cracker. Toast your marshmallow. Pull it off the stick and put it onto the chocolate. Put the second graham cracker on top, making a cracker-chocolate-marshmallow sandwich. Push the layers together so the marshmallow squishes and melts the chocolate.

Pudding

1 package (1.4 oz/39 g) vanilla instant pudding

1/2 cup (30 g) dried banana chips

1/2 cup (225 g) powdered milk

Mix the ingredients at home and put the mixture into a sealable bag. In camp, stir in as much water as the pudding instructions call for. Beat with a fork, pour it into four dishes or cups, and let the pudding set for at least 10 minutes.

You can invent many versions of this recipe. Try mini-chocolate chips in vanilla pudding, butter-scotch chips in chocolate pudding, coconut in banana pudding ... You get the idea. If it sounds good to you, try it.

OPERATING A COOKSTOVE

Set up your stove on a level surface so it doesn't tilt. Clear away twigs, leaves, and anything else that might burn. Stand on the side of the stove that faces the wind. You can also wrap a piece of aluminum foil around the stove to shield it.

HERE ARE 3 STOVE SAFETY TIPS:

- Pack your stove right-side up. Some stoves leak fuel if they're sideways or upside down.
- Store extra fuel several yards (meters) away from your tent.
- Never use a cookstove inside your tent. It puts out carbon monoxide, which can poison you if it builds up in a small space.

Save fuel by getting your food ready to cook or your pot of water ready to be boiled before you light the stove. Follow the directions that came with the stove for how to light it. Most stoves work like this:

- Pump up the pressure in the fuel tank.
- Open the valve that lets fuel flow to the burner.
- Hold a match to the burner (or click the electronic starter, if your stove has one). The stove will light.
- Turn the flow valve to the "run" position. There may be a second valve that lets you control the size of the flame.

MAKING A CAMPFIRE

A campfire is one of the best things about camping. Here is some information to help you build a campfire like a pro.

Make your fire small. Experienced campers know that big fires waste firewood. They spit out sparks that fly for many yards (meters), creating a fire danger to other campers and to the woods. A smaller fire is safer, easier to collect wood for, better for cooking, and a lot more fun to sit around.

FIREWOOD

Gather all the wood you think you'll need before you strike a match. Once the fire is burning, you shouldn't leave it to collect more wood. Without you there to tend it, it might go out. Or, it might spread and get out of control.

Collect dry, dead wood that is already on the ground. Don't cut branches off living trees. Gather from areas many yards (meters) from your campsite. If the site is used often by campers, good wood may be hard to find. Some campgrounds provide firewood to the campers.

Look for wood in sizes from twigs as thin as your finger to sticks as thick as your arm. Stack the wood at least 5 feet (1.5 m) from the fire ring. Arrange it in piles according to size. That way you can quickly grab what-ever size piece the fire needs.

Also gather smaller material, such as dry leaves, weeds, or pine needles. That's the tinder, or easy-to-burn material, you will use to help start your fire.

FIRE STARTERS

Sometimes tinder will burn well enough to get the bigger pieces of wood burning. Other times, tinder burns too fast. A fire starter will burn hot enough and long enough to get your campfire going great.

In dry weather, newspaper makes a great fire starter. Wad up a page very, very tightly. The tighter the ball, the longer it will burn. Make several newspaper balls before you start your fire. You will probably only use a few, but it's good to be prepared in case you need more.

Another kind of fire starter works in any kind of weather. Cotton fireballs are waterproof and they burn long and hot. Store them in a sealable sandwich bag or a plastic screw-top container.

BUILDING THE FIRE

Remove any trash and rocks that are in your fire ring.
Scoop out enough dirt to make a shallow pit wide enough
to hold your fire. Keep the dirt in a pile nearby. You
can use it to douse, or put out, your fire at the end
of the evening.

Place twigs in either a teepee or a log cabin arrange-
ment. Both styles work well. Try both, and find out
which works best for you.

Start with small twigs, and leave space between them.
Fire needs air. Don't pack your wood so tightly that the
fire can't "breathe."

Put your tinder or fire starters inside the teepee or log
cabin. Then light the fire. Regular matches usually work

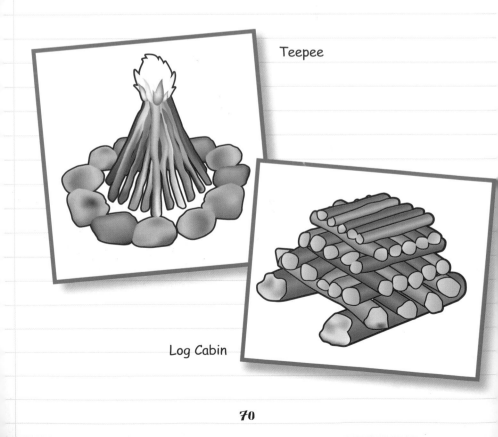

Teepee

Log Cabin

70

fine. If the wood smolders but doesn't burn, try blowing on it through a straw. Stay to one side of the fire, not above it, as you blow gently on the parts that are glowing.

When the fire "catches," keep a close eye on it. Feed it new wood before the flames die down. Use slightly thicker pieces of wood as the fire gets hotter. Your goal is to create a fire that will burn new wood that is added to it, eventually turning the wood into glowing coals.

If you make a teepee fire, add new wood so it points toward the center, like spokes on a wheel. As the sticks burn, push them in toward the center of the fire. If you make a log cabin fire, add new firewood crosswise to the previous layer. Always leave a gap where air can get to the center of the fire.

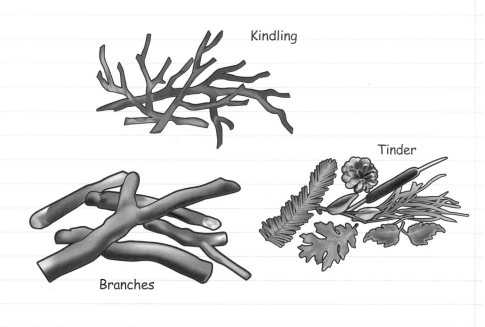

Kindling

Tinder

Branches

CHARCOAL FIRES

If wood is scarce or the weather is wet, you can use
charcoal briquets like the kind used in backyard bar-
becues. The briquets will be good for cooking on when
they have burned down to hot coals. If you cook on
them before then, your food can pick up a chemical
taste from oils in the briquets.

Charcoal

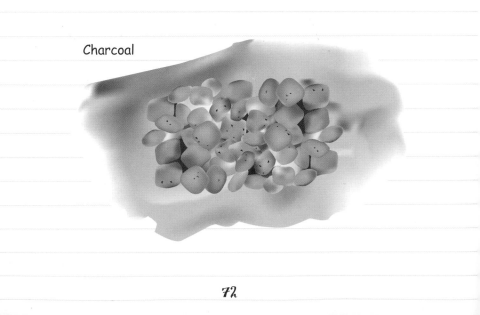

Before you leave your campfire, be sure it is completely out. You can douse it with water or dirt. Sand is better than crumbly soil.

Use a stick to stir the water or dirt into the coals. Then add more water or dirt. Stir again.

Carefully hold your hand close to the coals to find out if they are still hot. Don't pick up a coal! You might get burned.

If you feel heat coming off them, add more water or dirt. If they are cool, you can safely leave them.

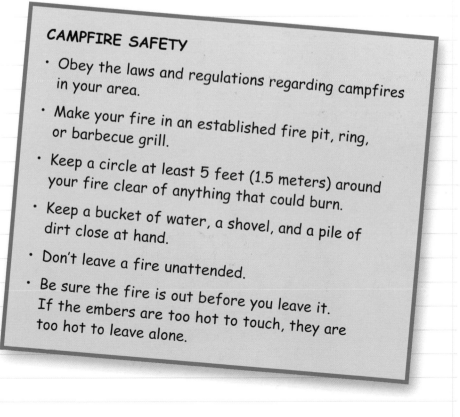

CAMPFIRE SAFETY

- Obey the laws and regulations regarding campfires in your area.
- Make your fire in an established fire pit, ring, or barbecue grill.
- Keep a circle at least 5 feet (1.5 meters) around your fire clear of anything that could burn.
- Keep a bucket of water, a shovel, and a pile of dirt close at hand.
- Don't leave a fire unattended.
- Be sure the fire is out before you leave it. If the embers are too hot to touch, they are too hot to leave alone.

COOKING IN CAMP

After your campfire has burned for about half an hour, it will be ready to cook your dinner. If you place a pan directly on the coals, be careful that it doesn't tip over. You can set a grill over the coals, and put your pan on that. If you're cooking sausages, hot dogs, or marshmallows, run a pointed stick through them and hold them over the coals to cook.

You'll have to experiment a bit to find out how high to turn the heat on your stove, or how close to the coals to place your food. If a pan heats up too fast, the food inside it will scorch. Watch closely, and stir the food often to keep it from sticking to the bottom of the pan. If it starts to burn, turn down the heat or move the pan farther from the coals.

CLEANING UP

Wash the dishes in your dishpan, using as little water and dish soap as you can. If you're in a campground, dump the dishwater in a marked drain. If you're in a campsite on your own, dump it on the ground several yards (meters) away from your tent. Use a
different spot every time you discard your dishwater.

If you have leftovers, save them in snap-top containers or burn them in the fire. Never leave food or trash around the campsite. It could attract dangerous animals such as bears, or encourage animals such as squirrels to depend on handouts from humans. And rotting food lying around makes the campsite unpleasant for the campers who come after you.

Put all of your trash into strong plastic bags. If the campground has a dumpster, put your trash there. If it doesn't, take the trash away with you. Don't pitch it in the first town you come to. Wait until you're at least 50 miles (80 km) away, and then put the trash in a dumpster.

BREAKING CAMP

When you break camp, make sure you have all your gear. It's easy to forget you left your sleeping bag airing out on a bush. One way to be sure you have everything is to use your camping checklist again.

Make sure your campsite will look just as good to the next camper as it did to you. Take out all of your trash. Don't leave cans or other garbage in the fire ring. If you had firewood left over, stack it neatly so the next campers can use it. Look at the site as if you were just arriving. Would you want to camp here? Try to leave the site looking the way you would want to find it.

"LEAVE NO TRACE"

Some campers do "leave no trace" camping. They try to leave no sign that they have camped in a place. They use only stoves, and do not build campfires. They pack out all solid wastes, including their own poops.

Many campers "leave little trace." They make fires and use latrines, but they are careful to have as little impact as they can. They camp in areas where people have camped before, not in areas that haven't been disturbed yet. They carry out all of their trash, and leave the campsite in better shape than it was when they arrived.

What Else Can I Do?

Whether you move camp every day or stay at one campsite, you'll have plenty of time to explore the animals, plants, rocks, and streams around you.

In this chapter, you will find some of the best things to do while camping.

ANIMAL WATCHING

Take binoculars for looking at animals that are hard to get close to, and a magnifying lens for looking at things extra-close-up.

Also take along field guides to the animals or plants you're most interested in. Field guides are books with pictures of the species you might see, and information about how each one lives. Many parks and National Forests have visitor centers where you can find out where to look for the animals.

Keep your eyes and ears open when you're in camp or on the trail. There's no thrill like seeing otters splashing in a river or hearing an owl screech in the woods.

If you're camping in an area where hummingbirds live and you're going to stay there for several days, try putting up a hummingbird feeder. Use a small one like the

kind people hang in their yards at home. Fill it with sugar water (put 1/4 cup/50 ml of sugar in a measuring cup, then add water to the 1-cup/250-ml mark). With luck, you'll be able to watch hummers get their breakfast while you are eating yours.

When you spot a creature, stay quiet and just point at your discovery. Your friends will know that means there's something special to look at. If you shout or wave your arms, you'll scare away the animals.

Even being quiet around animals sometimes won't let you sneak up on them. They will hear and smell you long before you see them. But if you're very quiet and respectful, they may let you look in on their lives. And that can be quite a show!

Remember that no matter how friendly wild animals look, they are not pets. They don't like people to get too close. If an animal moves away when you try to get closer to it, don't follow it. The animal may decide to turn around and fight.

HIKING

Hiking is the best way to explore the area around your camp. All you need are strong, comfortable shoes—cross-trainers or lightweight hiking shoes are perfect—and a small day pack. The pack you lug your school books around in will be fine. It's a good idea to wear a brightly colored shirt, especially during hunting season.

Take plenty of drinking water and a snack such as gorp or fruit roll-ups. Take a map of the trail, if you have one, and a field guide, binoculars, and a hand lens. Finally, just in case, take toilet paper, a rain jacket, waterproof matches, cotton fireballs, a whistle, and a flashlight. If you have room for a tarp, take that too. Oh, and the most important thing of all—take a friend!

Tell others where you are going, and stay on the trail. If you get turned around and think you might be lost, stop walking. Blow your whistle to attract attention. If you are with a buddy, stay together. Don't split up. Being lost is a lot scarier and more dangerous if you're alone.

FISHING

Fishing is great fun, plus it might bring you a delicious dinner of fresh fish. When you plan your camping trip, you can ask a forest ranger, campground host, or other fisherman what kind of fish live in the waters near your camp, and what kind of tackle (rods, reels, and lures) you will need.

TRASH ROUND-UP

Take a big plastic trash bag and make it your mission to pick up any pop cans, food wrappers, or other trash you find near camp or along a trail. You'll make the area nicer for yourself and other campers and know that you helped this beautiful area stay clean.

AROUND THE CAMPFIRE

Sitting around a campfire with friends is one of the best parts of camping. There are many fun things you can do.

SING

Even people who don't usually like to sing, enjoy singing around a campfire. You can sing fun songs like "Great Big Gobs of Greasy, Grimy Gopher Guts," traditional songs like "Home on the Range" or "Don't Fence Me In," spiritual songs like "Kumbayah," or any other song you feel like singing.

ROAST MARSHMALLOWS

While the fire is forming coals, prepare your marshmallow stick. It should be 3 to 4 feet (1 to 1.2 m) long and about 1 inch (2.5 cm) thick. With your pocket knife, strip the bark from the narrow end of the stick. Sharpen that end to a small point. If it has a branch near the end, sharpen both twigs. You'll have a double-decker stick!

Impale two or three big marshmallows on the sharpened point. Reach the stick out over the coals. Find just the right height for them. If they burst into flames, they're too close to the coals! When they're toasty brown all over, they're ready. They are very hot and will burn your mouth if you try to eat them right off the fire, so let them cool a bit. When they're cool enough to handle, slide them off the stick. You can use them to make S'mores, or just pop them in your mouth.

TELL STORIES

Sitting around a campfire is one of the best places in the world to tell and to hear stories. Exciting stories about explorers and pioneers in wild lands. Funny stories about camping mishaps. Scary stories about accidents and close calls. And most of all, ghost stories. There's something about being out in the woods, hearing sounds you're not used to, that makes spooky stories even scarier than usual.

Just remember, when you turn in for the night, that they are just stories somebody made up. Don't let them keep you awake. Snuggle into your sleeping bag in your safe, cozy tent, and dream about stories you can tell around the campfire next time.

WHAT IF IT RAINS?

Being stuck in your tent for a couple of days might seem like a disaster, but it isn't all bad. Here are some things you can do to make a rainy day in camp more fun.

GO GOURMET

A rainy day is one of the best times to try cooking a fancier meal than usual. The only tricky part is keeping the kitchen dry. If your campground has a picnic shelter, cook there. If it doesn't, rig a tarp to cover your cooking area.

READ OR WRITE

Rainy days are great times to read. You can lose your-self in stories about wilderness adventures or famous conservation heroes like John Muir or Rachel Carson.

Catch up on your journal or sketchbook or write a letter or postcard to a friend back home.

WHITTLE

When you get to camp, look for dry sticks you can use for whittling later on. Then, if it rains, you will have your raw materials all ready to work on. Use sticks you find on the ground. Don't break sticks off of living trees.

Try whittling a marshmallow-roasting stick or a figure of a bird or other animal.

Handle your knife with care. Always move the blade away from your body, and be sure your fingers aren't in its way. Whenever you stop whittling, even for a minute, fold up your knife so someone doesn't accidentally get cut.

PLAY GAMES

With a deck of cards you can play dozens of different games. You can also make your own games. One possibility is Animal Charades.

In this game, one camper imitates some animal. The other campers try to guess which animal it is. Let the person doing the imitating show you a whole "routine" of how the animal moves and what it sounds like, before anyone tries to guess what animal it is. Take turns being the "animal."

RECORD YOUR EXPERIENCE

Keep a journal of your camping adventures. Every day, write down what you did, what you ate, any problems that came up, and how you solved them. Your journal is the ideal place to jot down ideas for things to try on your next camping trip. A spiral-bound notebook "composition book" makes a good journal.

Camp is a great place to draw. If you'd rather draw than write, bring a sketchbook instead of a writing journal. Make a note on each drawing to remind yourself where and when you saw the thing you drew.

It's always fun to have photos of your trip to show friends and to relive the experience later. If you take a camera, be careful that it doesn't get wet or broken.

APPENDIX

Soon after you get home, clean your equipment so it will be ready for your next camping adventure. If you take care of your equipment, it will last for many years.

TENT

Gently shake your tent and fly and drape them over a clothesline to let them air out. Direct sunlight will damage the fabric, so place them in the shade. If they are dirty, use plain water and a sponge to remove the dirt.

BAG

Fluff up and air out your sleeping bag. Clean it once a year, or about once every 90 camping nights if you camp a lot. Check the label on the bag for instructions on how to clean it.

To carry a wet sleeping bag, wad it up in a bundle so the wet, heavy filling doesn't pull on the seams. Lay it open on a shady spot of ground. When it is partially dry, turn it over so the underside can dry.

TARP

Clean your tarps with water and a sponge. Let them dry in the shade before storing them. Fold them to about 3 feet (1 meter) wide, and then roll them up. Every time you stow a tarp, fold it a different way. Folds weaken the fibers, especially if the tarp is folded the same way every time.

WATER PURIFICATION SYSTEM

If you used a purifier, check your notes about how much water has gone through the filter. If the filter is due to be replaced, do that now so the purifier is ready to go the next time you are. If it doesn't need to be replaced yet, clean it by pumping through some water with bleach in it. Then rinse by pumping fresh tap water through it. Let the purifier and hoses air-dry. Then cover the tips of the hoses with plastic wrap to keep them clean during storage.

If you used iodine tablets, check the label to find out whether to keep this package until your next trip, or throw it out and start with a fresh package next time. Some iodine products don't last long after you open the bottle.

CAMPING CHECKLISTS

THINGS TO DO BEFORE EACH TRIP:

- Reserve a space in the campground, if necessary.

- Get field guides and a map of hiking trails or fishing spots near your campsite.

- Gather your gear. Use a checklist so you don't forget something important.

- Check the fuel supply for your stove.

- Plan your menu, gather the food, and store it in labeled containers.

THINGS TO DO EACH DAY OF THE TRIP:

- Air out your sleeping bag.

- Clean up after you cook and eat.

- Be sure the fire is out when you leave or go to sleep.

- Have fun!

THINGS TO DO AFTER EACH TRIP:

- Clean your tent, tarps, and sleeping pad.

- Air out your tent, fly, and sleeping bag before storing them.

- Change the filter in your water purifier if it's due; clean it with bleach if it can still be used.

THINGS TO DO ONCE A YEAR:

- Seal the seams on your tent and fly.

- Wash your sleeping bag.

NATIONAL PARKS

You can learn more information about the U.S. National Parks listed below, plus all the parks in your state, by visiting the National Park Sevice web site: www.nps.gov.

Acadia, ME

Arches, UT

Badlands, SD

Big Bend, TX

Biscayne, FL

Black Canyon of the Gunnison, CO

Bryce Canyon, UT

Canyonlands, UT

Capitol Reef, UT

Carlsbad Caverns, NM

Channel Islands, CA

Crater Lake, OR

Death Valley, NV, CA

Denali, AK

Dry Tortugas, FL

Everglades, FL

Gates of the Arctic, AK

Glacier, MT

Glacier Bay, AK

Grand Canyon, AZ

Grand Teton, WY

Great Basin, NV

Great Smoky Mtns, NC, TN

Guadalupe Mtns, TX

Haleakala, HI

Hawaii Volcanoes, HI

Hot Springs, AR

Isle Royale, MI

Joshua Tree, CA

Katmai, AK

Kenai Fjords, AK

King Canyon, CA

Kobuk Valley, AK

Lake Clark, AK

Lassen Volcanic, CA

Mammoth Cave, KY

Mesa Verde, CO

Mount Rainier, WA

North Cascades, WA

Olympic, WA

Petrified Forest, AZ

Redwood, CA

Rocky Mountain, CO

Saguaro, AZ

Sequoia, CA

Shenandoah, VA

Theodore Roosevelt, ND

Voyageurs, MN

Wind Cave, SD

Wrangell Saint Elias, AK

Yellowstone, ID, MT, WY

Yosemite, CA

Zion, UT

You can learn more information about the Canadian National Parks listed below, plus all the parks in your province, by visiting the Parks Canada web site: www.pc.gc.ca.

Aulavik, NT

Auyuittuq, NUN

Banff, AB

Bruce Peninsula, ON

Cape Breton Highlands, NS

Elk Island, AB

Ellesmere Island, NUN

Fathom Five, ON

Forillon, QC

Fundy, NB

Georgian Bay Islands, ON

Glacier, BC

Grasslands, SK

Gros Morne, NF

Gulf Islands, BC

Gwaii Haanas, BC

Ivvavik, YT

Jasper, AB

Kejimkujik, NS

Kluane, YT

Kootenay, BC

Kouchibouguack, NB

La Mauricie, QC

Mingan Archipelago, QC

Mount Revelstoke, BC

Nahanni, NT

Pacific Rim, BC

Point Pelee, ON

Prince Albert, SK

Prince Edward Island, PE

Pukaskwa, ON

Riding Mountain, MB

Saint Lawrence Islands, ON

Sirmilik, NUN

Terra Nova, NF

Tuktut Nogait, NT

Vuntut, YT

Wapusk, MB

Waterton Lakes, AB

Wood Buffalo, AB, NT

Yoho, BC

INDEX

Creative Publishing international
is your Complete Source of How-to Information for the Outdoors

Available Outdoor Titles:

Hunting Books
- Advanced Turkey Hunting
- Advanced Whitetail Hunting
- Bowhunting Equipment & Skills
- The Complete Guide to Hunting
- Dog Training
- Elk Hunting
- How to Think Like a Survivor
- Hunting Record-Book Bucks
- Mule Deer Hunting
- Muzzleloading
- Outdoor Guide to Using Your GPS
- Pronghorn Hunting
- Whitetail Hunting
- Whitetail Techniques & Tactics
- Wild Turkey

Fishing Books
- Advanced Bass Fishing
- The Art of Freshwater Fishing
- The Complete Guide to Freshwater Fishing
- Fishing for Catfish
- Fishing Rivers & Streams
- Fishing Tips & Tricks
- Fishing with Artificial Lures
- Inshore Salt Water Fishing
- Kids Gone Fishin'
- Largemouth Bass
- Live Bait Fishing
- Modern Methods of Ice Fishing
- Northern Pike & Muskie
- Offshore Salt Water Fishing
- Panfish

- Salt Water Fishing Tactics
- Smallmouth Bass
- Striped Bass Fishing: Salt Water Strategies
- Successful Walleye Fishing
- Trout
- Ultralight Fishing

Fly Fishing Books
- The Art of Fly Tying
- The Art of Fly Tying – CD ROM
- Complete Photo Guide to Fly Fishing
- Complete Photo Guide to Fly Tying
- Fishing Dry Flies – Surface Presentations for Trout in Streams
- Fly-Fishing Equipment & Skills
- Fly Fishing for Beginners
- Fly Fishing for Trout in Streams
- Fly-Tying Techniques & Patterns

Cookbooks
- All-Time Favorite Game Bird Recipes
- America's Favorite Fish Recipes
- America's Favorite Wild Game Recipes
- Babe & Kris Winkelman's Great Fish & Game Recipes
- Backyard Grilling
- Cooking Wild in Kate's Camp
- Cooking Wild in Kate's Kitchen
- Dressing & Cooking Wild Game
- The New Cleaning & Cooking Fish
- Preparing Fish & Wild Game
- Recipes from Nature
- The Saltwater Cookbook
- Venison Cookery

To purchase these or other Creative Publishing international titles,
contact your local bookseller, or visit our website at
www.creativepub.com